How the Summer Season Came

and Other Assiniboine Indian Stories

How the Summer Season Came

and Other Assiniboine Indian Stories

Published by the
Montana Historical Society Press
in cooperation with the
Fort Peck and Fort Belknap Tribes

HELENA, MONTANA

Originally published as *How the Summer Season Came, Assiniboine Woman Making Grease, Duckhead Necklace and Indian Love Story, How the Big Dipper and the North Star Came to Be,* and *Ghost Stories* in the Indian Reading Series by the Pacific Northwest Indian Program, Joseph Coburn, Director, Northwest Regional Educational Laboratory, Portland, Oregon

Cover drawing by George Shields, Jr.
Cover design by DD Dowden, Helena

Revised edition copyright © 2003 by Fort Peck Tribal Library, Fort Peck Community College, P.O. Box 398, Poplar, Montana 59255

Distributed by the Globe Pequot Press, 246 Goose Lane, Guilford, Connecticut 06437, (800) 243-0495

Library of Congress Cataloging-in-Publication Data:
How the summer season came : and other Assiniboine Indian stories.
    p. cm.
Summary: A collection of six traditional tales collected at Fort Peck reservation in northern Montana, which were originally intended to teach young members of the tribe about their history and culture.
ISBN 0-917298-94-2 (pbk. : alk. paper)
1. Assiniboine Indians—Folklore. 2. Tales—Montana—Fort Peck Indian Reservation.
3. Legends—Montana—Fort Peck Indian Reservation. [1. Assiniboine Indians—Folklore.
2. Indians of North America—Montana—Folklore. 3. Folklore—Montana.]
E99.A84H696 2003
398.2'089'9752—dc21

                    2003044591

How the Summer Season Came and *Duckhead Necklace and Indian Love Story* copyright © 1981 by the Fort Belknap Indian Community, Gros Ventre and Assiniboine Tribes

Assiniboine Woman Making Grease copyright © 1978 Assiniboine and Sioux Tribes of the Fort Peck Reservation

How the Big Dipper and North Star Came to Be and "True Story of a Ghost" copyright © 1981 Assiniboine and Sioux Tribes of the Fort Peck Reservation

This project was funded by an Enhancement Grant from the
Institute of Museum and Library Services awarded
to Fort Peck Tribal Library in 2001.
Additional funding was provided by
Assiniboine and Sioux Enterprise Community

CONTENTS

How the Summer Season Came

By members of the Assiniboine Elders
Board of the Fort Belknap Reservation
Researched by Kenneth E. Ryan
Illustrated by George Shields, Jr.

A long time ago, the Assiniboine people lived in a part of the country that was almost always covered by snow. There were no horses, and only dogs were used to carry things. A small war party returned after being gone a long time and went to the chief's lodge. They told the chief to call the Council together because they had an important message. The chief fed the war party and sent his camp crier to call all Council members to his lodge.

The spokesman from the war party said, "We have been away from our people for many moons. We have set foot on land that belongs to others, a land without snow.

This land is in the direction where the sun rests at midday. In the middle of a large encampment there is a lodge painted yellow. Within the lodge the summer is kept in a bag hung on a tripod. Four old men guard it day and night. One sits in the back, directly under the tripod. Another lies across the entrance and two others sit on each side by the fireplace."

The chief and his headmen sat in the Council until one of them said, "Let us call in a representative from each of the fast-running animals. We will ask them to help us bring this wonderful thing to our country." The camp crier went forth and called upon those medicine men who had fast-running animals and invited them all to the lodge.

During the Council the chief said, "My people and my animal others, far in the direction of midday there is the summer. I call you here to make plans to bring it to our people. Those chosen to go will never come back alive, but they will do a great service to our people and to their kind. Their children will enjoy the breath of summer forever." It was decided to send the lynx, the red fox, the antelope, the coyote and the wolf.

The young warriors who knew the way were to guide the summer back to the encampment. After many days of marching they arrived near the camp where summer was kept, and they took council. The spokesman said, "The lynx will go into the lodge and bring out the bag containing the summer because no one can hear him walk. He will give it to the red fox who will be waiting for him along the way. From there the antelope will carry it to the coyote. The coyote will take it to the wolf

who is long-winded and he will bring it to us by the big river. We will be waiting on the opposite bank for him. From there we will take it to our people." The lynx was sent to the lodge.

The red fox was told to take his position. All the animals were stationed a certain distance apart according to the ability of the runner. If an animal was short-winded, it was not required to make a long run. The bag was to be carried at the fastest speed. Toward morning before the light showed and everyone in the camp was asleep, the lynx softly walked to the yellow lodge and looked in. The four old men guarding the summer were all asleep. The bag containing the summer was hanging on the tripod in the back part of the lodge. The summer was in the form of spring water and moved about in a bag made from the stomach of a buffalo. Now and then the bag overflowed and water trickled along the ground under the tripod. Where the water fell on the ground green grass and many different kinds of plants and flowers grew.

Cautiously, on quiet feet the lynx entered
stepping carefully over the entrance. With
a quick jerk he snapped the cord that
held the bag. Seizing it tightly in his
teeth he plunged through the door
and sped away. Almost at the same
instant the four old men awakened and
gave the alarm. "The summer has been
stolen!" The cry went from lodge to
lodge. In a short time a group of
horsemen on fast horses were after the lynx.

They were gaining rapidly on the lynx when he gave
the bag to the red fox who was waiting for him.

The horsemen then killed the lynx
and started after the fox who, after a
time, gave the bag to the antelope.

The antelope took the bag to the coyote, who brought it
to the wolf. Wolf, the long-winded one, was to deliver it
to the waiting party. Each time the bag was passed from
a winded runner to the next the animal was killed by
the pursuers.

As the wolf crossed the river the ice began to move and break up. By the time the horsemen reached the river, it was flowing ice. This halted the horsemen from the south. In sign language they said to the Assiniboine, "Let us bargain with each other for the possession of summer." After a time it was decided that each would keep summer for six moons.

After six moons it was to be taken back to the river and delivered to the waiting party. The arrangement was kept, allowing summer half of the year in each country. The bargain gave two seasons, the winter and the summer.

After many winter and summer years had passed, the headmen of the Assiniboine decided to have the cranes carry the summer back and forth. The cranes were always the first migratory fowl to go south. They migrated in easy stages, stopping for long periods at good feeding grounds.

If that method was used for carrying summer, the winter would gradually make its appearance. This method would be better than when the summer was taken south by the men. The fall season, Pda Yedu, made its appearance gradually.

Long before the cranes returned north, there were signs among the plants and animals that the summer was on its way. That time was called the spring, Wedu. A late fall or spring was a sign the cranes had found good feeding grounds and stayed around them longer. An early winter or summer was a sign the cranes had winged their way south or north too soon. When the cranes flew over an encampment, they always circled several times and with their loud calls seem to proclaim their arrival and departure.

With the cranes help the Assiniboine had four seasons: Winter—Waniydin, Summer—Mno Gedu, Fall—Pda Yedu, and Spring—Wedu.

Assiniboine Woman
Making Grease

As told by Jerome Fourstar
Illustrated by Joseph Clancy

Long ago, a favorite camp site of the Assiniboines was south of the present Jack Norris Coulee. It is 22 miles north of Frazer on the little Porcupine Creek.

This was a large encampment. The hunters hunted buffalo in a radius of about twenty miles.

When the hunters brought in buffalo, the women prepared much of the meat for winter by drying it.

They would cut the meat into thin slices. These slices were hung on a rack. A smudge fire was built under the meat. The fire did not cook the meat; instead, the smoke kept flies and other insects away from the meat while it was drying.

It also provided a pleasant taste to the meat. Once the meat was dry, it could be stored for several months.

The buffalo hide was also prepared by the women. To prepare the hide, it was first stretched and pegged to the ground. After some drying, the hide was scraped by elkhorn scrapers to remove the hair and the fat. The fat was then rendered into grease.

The grease was rubbed into the hide on both sides and allowed to soak into the hide. After a day or two, the hide was softened by pulling it back and forth around a pole that stands upright. After the hide was softened, the tanned hide was ready for use.

Game became scarce and it was decided that the camp would move. Scouts had located a place where game was abundant. Everyone began packing to move.

An old woman in the camp was not ready to move because she was in the process of making grease. She told
the others, "Go on. I am
going to stay and finish
before I follow you."

That night she was finishing the rendering of the grease. Because she did not have lights to work with, she took a long willow and made it into a torch. The torch was made by dipping one end into grease and lighting it. She took the unlighted end and pushed it down the back of her dress. This gave her light to work by.

The old woman heard some sounds outside. She looked out and saw eight enemy warriors. She was sure they were planning to kill her. She thought of an idea to escape. She put some green wood on her fire and invited the warriors in to eat pemmican.

The warriors accepted her invitation and came inside. The green wood was beginning to fill the inside with smoke. She told them she was going outside to open the flaps of the tepee to let the smoke out. Once outside, she began running toward a high cliff.

When she didn't return, one of the warriors looked out. He spotted her immediately because she still had the torch on her back. The young warrior told the others, "She's getting away!" They all ran after her.

The old woman led them toward the high cliff. As they got closer, she threw the torch over the cliff. She ran to the side and hid.

The warriors did not know the cliff was there. They were running as fast as they could toward the light and went over the edge of the cliff.

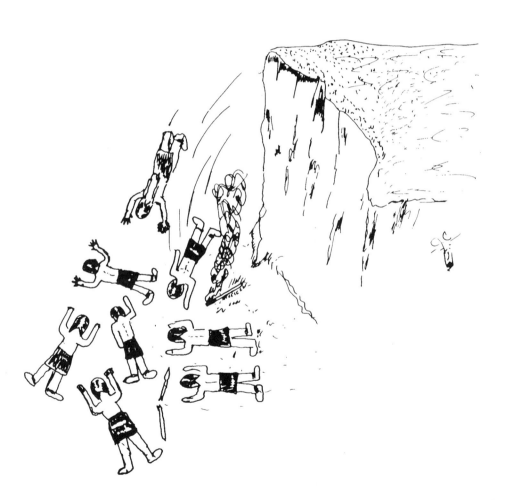

The next day, the old woman packed up and joined the main camp. She told the chiefs, "I have killed eight enemy warriors." She told them her story.

The chiefs did not believe her, and they went to the cliff to see for themselves. Sure enough, all eight enemy warriors were dead at the bottom of the cliff.

The old woman became a heroine!

Indian Love Story

Narrated and illustrated by George Shields, Sr.

This is a true story. It happened hundreds of years ago, back in the days of the buffalo when the Indians roamed this country freely.

In those days Indian people of different tribes did not understand each other's language. They fought each other some of the time. The fighting brought honor to the victor. An Indian who earned many coups from his enemy was considered a chief. What the white man calls a horse thief, long ago was considered honorable in the Indian society. The Indians made horse raids and advised the younger people who had horses not to be sleepy heads. "If you sleep late and don't wake up at night, you are going to go around by foot. You won't have any horses if you sleep too long. You will be easy prey for enemies."

There was a young Indian man who was the only child of a married couple. He met a young Indian girl who was one of two children. The young man fell in love with this young girl. They talked of love but never touched each other. They would stand many feet apart, just close enough to hear what was being said to each other.

Time went on and there was to be a war party. The young man wanted to see his sweetheart before he left. After sundown he went to his girlfriend's camp. He went near her tepee and the girl came out. She waited to hear what he had to say. The young man said, "I came to tell you that tomorrow night a war party is leaving. I want to go. I want to make something of myself. When I come back we will talk to our parents and perhaps we can marry." While the man was talking the girl never said anything. She just bowed her head.

After he stopped talking the girl said, "Is that all you wanted to tell me?"

The young man said, "Yes."

"Listen," she said, "you are suggesting you want honor so people will recognize you, maybe as a chief. Why do you want that? Your father is a great chief, a respected man. People respect you as much as they respect your father. You don't have to go. Some people who go on war parties never come back. What if that happens to you? What's going to happen to me? My heart and my beliefs are for you. My love is for you. If I lose you I'm nothing. I don't think I will go on living. I love you that much. I don't want you to go. You don't need anything else than what you have now. You are respected already. You ride good horses. You wear good clothes. You have plenty to eat. You live in a good tepee with your father and mother. What more do you want?"

The man said, "I know but that isn't enough for me. I want a name for myself before I ask for a wife. I just have to go."

They argued back and forth. Finally, the girl gave up. She never said anything. She just stood there and hung her head. It was dark so the young man could not see if the girl was crying.

He went to his tepee and put on a good robe fixed with porcupine quillwork. It was fancy, one of the best robes. He took the robe back to the girl "I'm going to go," he said. "While I'm gone I want you to keep this. When I come back I want to see this blanket and you. We will get married if our parents consent."

He left. He didn't kiss her, because they didn't do that in those days. The girl just stood there while he disappeared into the darkness.

The next night the war party went looking for their enemy. They found them and fought. The young man killed an enemy and took his scalp and other things for coups. They won the fight and started back. The return trip took many days.

One day they approached an old camp, the same camp they had left some days before. The young man began looking around the campsite. He walked to the river and came back saying, "I found something. While we were gone someone must have died. The person was buried in a tepee in the woods over there."

The young man felt uneasy about talking about someone
who had passed away. "I'll go over there and look," he
said. When he came to the side of the tepee, his heart fell
but he didn't cry. The tepee was staked down solid all
around. The doorway was entwined with sticks so
wolves, or coyotes could not get inside the tepee and eat
the dead person. He undid all the twigs and sticks and
peeked inside. As soon as he stuck his head inside the
doorway he recognized his blanket. There his sweetheart
lay dead, covered with the blanket. When he saw this he
wanted to make sure. He went over to the body and
uncovered the face. Sure enough, it was his sweetheart.
He went back to his war party.

He said, "The dead person is the girl who told me not to go on the war party. It is the girl I promised to marry when I came back. She told me if I didn't listen to her and stay, she would die of loneliness. She told the truth. She died because of me. I'm the one who caused it. I'm going to stay here with her. She's a woman and she's out here all by herself. I'm a man and I should be with her."

A wise man in the war party said, "No, don't do that. She's been gone for a long time. Come back with us. These things happen. If you stay here you can't bring her back. It's just going to be harder on you."

But the young man just wouldn't accept it.

Finally, the wise man said, "All right then. You stay but don't harm yourself because of her. She's in the happy hunting grounds with the rest of her relatives who have gone before her."

"No, I won't do anything. I just want to stay with her for four days," the young man said. "Take the horses and the scalp that I have and give them to my father. Tell him what I am doing and that I'm going to come back."

The men left him and he went back to the camp, the burial grounds. He went inside the tepee and crawled in beside his sweetheart. The man's body touched her dead body as he lay there. The first night he didn't sleep a wink. The second night he was able to sleep a little and the third night he slept well. The fourth night he slept soundly. That morning he heard movement inside the tepee and a fire was burning. The burning fire was crackling. He just lay there because he thought he was dreaming.

Suddenly, he heard a woman's voice. "Get up. You're going to eat," she said. Still he lay there. He still thought he was dreaming. Again the woman spoke and the third time he opened his eyes. There was a fire in the middle of the tepee. There was also food cooking. His sweetheart was sitting by the fire.

She said, "My folks sent me some food and we are going to eat. But before we eat I want to tell you this. I told you what was going to happen. Now you sleep by me. You don't fear me. You don't hate me. I pitied you. After we eat we're going home to your people, my people." She looked like she did when she was alive. She had good clothes and nicely combed hair. After they ate she said, "When we go out, fix this doorway the way you found it. Fix it so no animal can get in here."

They went to find their families. They traveled day after day. Finally the girl asked, "Are you hungry?"

The young man said, "Yes, I'm hungry now."

"Well, do you see that herd of buffalo over there? Go over there and kill a fat young buffalo. They won't see you because I will give you my power," she said. He killed the buffalo. They cut out the best parts and cooked them.

Their journey home continued day after day. The summer sky was clear. The grass was green and trees by the river were covered with green leaves. Every now and then they saw a herd of buffalo. The buffalo would not pay any attention to them. They could not see them because the young woman gave the man special power.

They continued to travel until one day they came upon a high ridge. Far below by a river was a large camp. The girl said, "Here are our people. Our parents live in this camp. We are going down there but I want you to go to your parent's place. That is where you belong anyway."

They started down the ridge to the camp. As soon as they came close to the encampment all the dogs barked and barked. They smelled something and ran in the opposite direction. The dogs knew a soul was coming alongside the young man. That was why they barked. The people felt strange. A man was coming and the dogs were barking at him. The dogs had never done that before.

The young man went to his parent's tepee. His mother was very glad to see him. She hung onto her son and cried. She said, "My son, I'm glad you came back. We heard what you did and we were scared. Our enemies are still nearby. I'm glad you came back. Sit down and drink some water. I will feed you." He sat down on his bed. His parents had fixed it just like he had been sleeping on it.

When he sat down, his sweetheart sat down beside him. The people could not see her because a soul cannot be seen by a living person. The young man's mother began to feed him. "Your father just killed a young buffalo and we have good meat," she said. She fed him and put some water beside the food. Before he ate, he took the water and food and put it beside him in front of the girl. He continued talking to his parents and after awhile he took the food and ate it. Every time they fed him he did that. He wouldn't touch the food and water until he placed it on his left side. His mother noticed the strange way he was acting.

One day after the young man had gone outside, his father came in. The mother said, "Our son has been acting very strangely. He never acted like this before. I have noticed his strange ways since he came back."

After awhile the young man came back to his mother's tepee. The girl's soul went wherever he went. His mother said, "My son, you've been acting very strangely. Tell us, why you are acting like this?"

The young man said, "Mother, the girl that passed away at the old camp is with me. She's right here." When he said that, the girl smiled. After that his mother set two places, one for the girl's soul and one for her son. When his mother did this the girl was very happy.

The young man would eat everything, but the girl's food was always left uneaten. Time went on until a war party was getting ready to leave.

The girl said to the young man, "You have to make a name for yourself so we must go along. You said you liked horses. It is time to get some." They went in broad daylight and took horses from the enemy. It was as if the horses strayed off by themselves. No one could see the man because the girl gave him the power to be invisible. He made many horse raids, each time getting many horses. He became a great chief.

The girl's soul stayed with the young man for four years. One day the girl said, "I promised I would live with you for four years. Now four years are up and everything you have been wishing for on this earth you now have. I cannot stay longer than I promised so this is the end. I have a sister. She is a very beautiful woman. I want you to marry her and always be good to her. She will take my place. I want you to love my sister as much as you have loved me. You and she are going to have a very good life from this day on. Take my sister as your wife and always respect her." The young man told his mother what the girl had said. His mother went to the girl's parents and talked with them. They were willing and happy.

"These are our departed daughter's words and we cannot refuse them. We will do as she wishes." They had a big gathering among the young man's relatives and friends, as well as the bride's relatives and friends. Both families exchanged gifts. The couple was married by an old warrior who performed the ceremony. They lived a long and happy life.

How the Big Dipper and North Star Came to Be

As told by Jerome Fourstar
Illustrated by Joseph Clancy

Long ago monsters roamed the earth and hunted for people to eat. At that time there lived seven brothers. These brothers lived in a big tepee far in the forest near a lake.

The brothers shared many things, even cooking and hunting chores. Whenever the brothers went hunting, one or two remained at home to take care of the tepee and do the cooking.

One day while the youngest brother was out hunting, he got a buffaloberry thorn caught in his hand. No matter

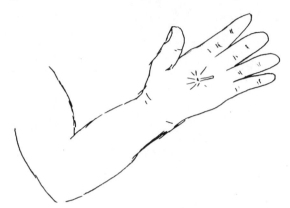

how hard he tried, he couldn't get the thorn out. Soon his hand began to swell and hurt.

The following morning, the youngest brother stayed home while the rest of the brothers went hunting. His hand still hurt, so he decided to wash it and see if the thorn would come loose. While he was washing his hand a little girl popped out instead of the thorn.

He was so surprised! He took the little girl and put her under his pillow. When his brothers returned, he didn't tell them what had happened. Finally, the oldest brother asked about his hand. He told everyone what had happened.

Everyone wanted to see the little girl. The youngest brother carefully took the little girl from behind his pillow and showed his brothers what she looked like.

After seeing the little girl the oldest brother said, "We will keep her and raise her like our own daughter."

When the little girl began to walk, the oldest brother gave her a beaver for a pet. Soon twelve moons had passed and the girl had grown into a teenager.

During the next six moons the girl learned many things. Before long the girl knew how to tan hides and make clothes. She even made a bigger tepee for her seven fathers.

One day the oldest brother told the girl to always be careful because monsters roamed about looking for people to eat. "The monsters try to fool people by telling them that they are cold and hungry. If you hear monsters you must not open the tepee flap, even if you feel sorry for them," the oldest brother told the girl.

The girl stayed inside the tepee and continued to do her chores while the brothers went hunting. The beaver stayed with the girl and kept her company.

One day while the girl was alone, she heard a voice out-side saying, "I'm cold and hungry." The girl heard foot-steps walking around the tepee. Thinking there was a real person outside, she opened the tepee to take a peek.

It was a monster! The monster grabbed her by the wrist and pulled her outside. "Come on," the monster said, "I'm taking you home with me." The girl told the mon-ster to wait so she could bring her beaver. The monster yelled, "Hurry and get it. We have a long way to go."

The monster took the girl to the lake where he had his boat. He pushed the girl and her beaver into the boat. The monster took a stick and hit the boat saying, "All right boat, let's get going." Soon the boat was moving across the lake. After a while the monster again hit the boat and this time he told the boat to go faster. The boat went as fast as it could.

It was sundown when they arrived at the
monster's house. The monster told the
girl to get out of the boat and go inside.
The monster hollered to his
grandmother,
"Come see
what I
brought
home."

When the monster's grandmother came out, the
monster said, "Look what I brought for us to eat. She is a
little on the skinny side. We will keep her and fatten her
up first." The monster told his grandmother to keep an
eye on the girl so she would not run away.

"I will sleep outside." He made his bed by the door in case the girl tried to sneak away. She would wake him up if she tried to jump over him.

During the next week the monster went hunting for other people even though he still kept the girl captive. Every time the monster returned, he was always empty-handed. Finally, one day as the monster was leaving to go hunting, he told the grandmother, "Kill the girl. She is fat enough. We will have her for supper."

After the monster left the grandmother told the girl, "You must kill me and cook me instead. When you cook me save my arm. Take a hatchet and put my arm far in the forest. Then you must leave as quickly as possible. Run towards the morning sun and you will come to a creek. You must cross the creek and run along the edge of the forest. Soon you will come to a house that looks like a tepee, but this house will be as hard as stone. Knock on the door and someone will help you."

The girl put the old lady in the pot and began to cook her. She put a lot of wood in the fire so the pot would boil. Taking the old lady's arm, hatchet, and her pet beaver, she headed for the woods.

When she was far away, she put a hatchet in the arm's hand and left it under a tree.

The girl ran through the woods as fast as she could. She ran in the direction the old lady had told her. Soon she came to the creek but could not cross it because the banks were too steep. The girl didn't know what to do.

After thinking for a while, she remembered her pet beaver could gnaw on the tree and cut it down. The beaver made the tree fall by his gnawing. The tree landed across the creek and made a bridge.

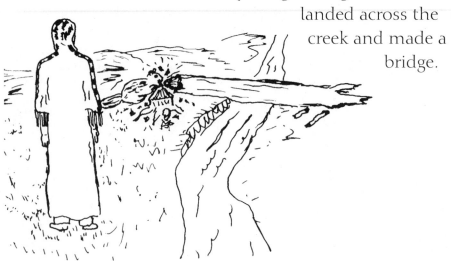

Once the girl crossed the creek, the beaver
followed her. When they reached the forest,
they ran along the edge. She
didn't know
how far they
would have
to run. They
kept on
going as fast
as they could.

When the monster returned home, he hollered to his
grandmother, "I'm home. Where is my
dinner?" The monster saw the pot of
stew boiling on the fire and decided to
start eating. Again the monster called
to his grandmother but still she did
not answer.

As the monster ate he heard chopping sounds coming from the woods. The monster thought his grandmother was out chopping more wood for the fire. The monster called for her to come and eat, but the chopping sounds continued. After the monster tasted the stew he said, "This stew smells and tastes like an old lady." The monster decided to go look for his grandmother. He began walking toward the chopping noise.

When he reached the tree where the girl had left the arm and hatchet, he saw his grandmother's arm. The monster knew the girl had run away. "I will follow her because I can smell her scent!" the monster shouted.

About this time the girl had finally reached the big tepee house that was as hard as stone. She knocked on the door and asked for help. Just as the door was being opened, the girl heard the monster coming from the woods. "Please hurry! There is a monster after me," the girl cried.

When the door opened the man inside the house saw the monster too, but the monster reached the girl. "Let the girl go!" the monster shouted to the man. "She's mine!"

The man went inside and came
out with two large
mountain lions.
He let the lions
go and they
attacked the
monster. The
man took the
girl inside and
told her the
mountain
lions were his pets. He also told her she would be all
right now that the monster was gone.

After the girl had stayed with the man for many months,
he told her, "You have been away from home for a long
time. Your seven fathers still miss you. They think you
are dead. I think it is time for you to return home." The
man had magic powers and he could
turn himself into an eagle. "I will
take you home. While you
walk, I will fly
overhead and
guide you."

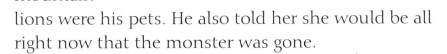

The next day, the man changed into an eagle. He stayed with the girl until they arrived at her home. When the eagle knew the girl was safe, he flew back to his home and changed back into a man.

The girl peeked inside the tepee and saw her seven fathers sitting with their heads bowed. She pushed her beaver inside the tepee. When the brothers saw the beaver they shouted and were happy. They welcomed their daughter and gave thanks that she was safe.

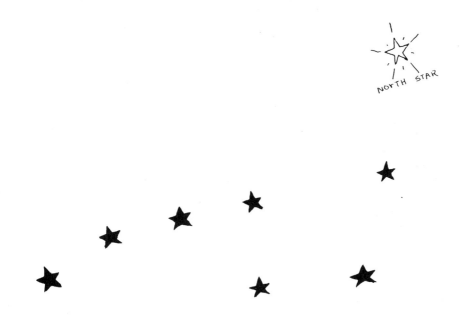

NORTH STAR

The next morning the oldest of the brothers said, "My daughter, we must protect you from the monsters that roam the earth. To do this we will go up to the sky. From this day on we will be the Big Dipper and you will be the North Star. Whenever people look into the sky at night, they will see you and they will not get lost." Together the brothers and the girl flew to the sky. There they stayed, safe from all the monsters on earth.

True Story of a Ghost

As told by Jerome Fourstar
Illustrated by Joseph Clancy

A GHOST IS A SPIRIT OF SOMEONE WHO HAS DIED and is earth-bound. This story is about a ghost who chased four teenage boys. It happened long before the white man came.

The Plains Indians buried their dead by placing the body on a scaffold. It was customary to bury the person with their most valuable possessions.

A man had died and he was buried in the traditional way of the Plains Indians. At the same time the burial was taking place, there was a celebration going on about eight miles away.

At the celebration were four teenage boys. The oldest boy
was about sixteen. Although they were all having a good
time at the celebration, the oldest boy wanted to leave
and ride out to the burial grounds. He was curious about
the dead man's belongings. He really didn't want to go
alone and he knew his friends would never agree to go
there with him. It was a scary place and it would be a
long ride to get home before dark.

He decided to make up a story about going hunting.
He knew his friends would leave the celebration for
that. They all liked to hunt and they would be anxious
to go along.

The boys left the celebration and rode their horses toward the burial grounds. The oldest boy did not tell them where they were going. He just told them they would hunt in a secret place. The boys rode along and did not ask any questions. They took their time and only walked their horses.

Soon they arrived at the burial grounds. The boys were surprised. They had been tricked into going there. The younger boys didn't like being there. They were scared and wanted to leave.

The oldest boy said, "We have come this far. Let's look at the dead man and see what valuables he has."

The younger boys protested, "We better leave now. It will be dark before we get home and we will all be in trouble!"

The oldest boy paid no attention and climbed onto the scaffold where the dead man was lying. He was surprised to see all the valuable belongings the dead man had. He decided to take them for himself and his friends. He then gave each of his friends some of the dead man's things.

The boys were scared and didn't want to keep them. The oldest boy said, "The man is dead and has no use for them. Go ahead and keep them." The older boy was about to climb down when he saw the dead man's Sun Dance whistle around his neck.

The younger boys were scared and anxious to leave. They were already on their horses and called to the older boy to hurry up.

The older boy climbed down, got on his horse, and they all started back to the celebration.

They had ridden a short distance when one of the boys felt very nervous and uneasy. He felt like someone was watching them. He nervously looked back toward the burial ground and was terrified at what he saw. The dead man was climbing down off the scaffold! He shouted to the others, "Look! Look!" When the other boys looked they too saw the dead man. Shaking and scared, they wanted to get away as fast as they could. The dead man was heading straight for them.

The boys made their horses run faster but it didn't help. No matter how fast they went, the dead man was getting closer. They couldn't get away. They ran their horses hard but it was not use. The dead man was gaining.

One of the boys yelled, "He wants his things. Give them back!" The boys began throwing the belongings to the ground.

When the dead man reached the spot where his things were, he stopped and looked at them. He started after them again even faster. He was getting closer and closer. The older boy realized he still had the Sun Dance whistle around his neck. He threw it down so hard it broke into many pieces.

When the dead man got to the spot where the oldest boy threw his whistle, he stopped and picked up all the pieces. He stood for a moment staring at all the pieces. Then he turned and slowly walked back toward the burial ground.

The boys and their horses were exhausted. Their hearts were still pounding but they felt safe and continued back to the celebration at a slower pace.

It had been a long and frightening day. Since it was getting late they decided to go straight home. When the boys arrived home, they went their separate ways to their own tepees and went to bed.

During the night the oldest boy woke up. He heard strange sounds. It sounded like people crying and praying. He was so tired he fell back to sleep. He didn't wake up again until morning. When he awoke he knew something was wrong. His parents told him, "One of your friends died during the night." He wondered if it had something to do with taking the things from the dead man.

The following night he heard the sounds again. People were crying and praying. In the morning his parents told him, "Another of your friends has died during the night." The boy was very scared now that two of his friends were dead.

On the third night it happened again. There were sounds of people crying and praying in the night and news in the morning that another friend had died. The boy was scared because he knew he would be next. He knew the dead man's spirit was getting even with them for taking his things.

Tonight would be his night to die. As the boy got ready for bed he prepared for his own death. He put on his good buckskin clothes and his best moccasins. He didn't think anything or anyone could help him now.

He thought of painting his face red to keep away the bad spirits but it seemed too late for even that. He didn't want to die and decided to use the red paint anyway. It was worth a try. As he was putting the paint on, he had many thoughts. He felt he was to blame for his friends' deaths. How wrong he had been to take things that didn't belong to him. He was sad and sorry for what he had done.

When the sun rose next morning the boy's father shook him to wake him up. When the boy woke his father said, "Why are you wearing your good buckskin clothes and your best moccasins?" The boy was surprised to be alive but he was very glad. He told his father about he and his three friends leaving the celebration to visit the burial ground.

"I tricked my friends into going with me. When we got there we took many of the dead man's belongings," he said. He told his father how the dead man had chased them. It didn't matter how fast they made their horses run, the dead man continued to follow them. The boy described how his friends had thrown the dead man's belongings on the ground but he still followed them. The boy said, "I finally realized the Sun Dance whistle I had taken from him was still around my neck. I threw it to the ground and the dead man finally stopped chasing us."

The boy's father told him the reason he didn't die was because he painted his face red. "The dead man's spirit had come for you but when he saw the red paint he knew you were sorry and had learned about feelings and respect for others. The dead man let you live so you could tell the story to others," said the boy's father.

The young man learned a valuable lesson. This story has been told many times to remind everyone they must always respect the people who have died, as well as respect their possessions.

Duckhead Necklace

Narrated by Isabel Shields
Illustrated by George Shields, Sr.

One evening two Indian girls sat outside looking at the stars. One star was very bright. "I wish that bright star would come down and marry me," one of the girls said. The next evening a young Indian man came from an opening in the sky. He was a handsome and nicely dressed man. He took the young girl back with him into the sky and they were married.

He took her to live in a very beautiful place. She was happy and enjoyed everything. There were many things for her to do. She could do anything she wanted but there was one exception. She was told not to dig large green turnips. After a while she became lonesome. She took long walks looking for the hole in the sky. One day she realized she was to have a baby. This made her even more homesick.

On one of her walks she found some big green turnips. Even though she was told not to, she dug one up. It left a large hole. She looked down and saw the place where she used to live. She made plans to go back. Every time her husband brought game home she tanned only part of the hide. She cut the rest of the hide into strips and dried them to make a rawhide rope. She was trying to hurry as it was almost time to have her baby and she wanted to be home when the baby was born.

GEO. SHIELDS

When she thought she had enough rawhide, she tied the strips together and made a long rope. Once the rope was finished she went to the hole. She tied one end of the rope to a rock and the other end around her waist. Slowly she let herself down through the hole. The rope wasn't long enough and she was left hanging in mid-air.

When her husband came home he discovered she was missing. He looked everywhere. Finally, he discovered the hole in the sky. There he found her hanging at the end of the rawhide rope. He picked up a rock and said, "Split her in two but don't hurt the baby." He threw the rock down and hit the woman. She fell to the ground and died. The baby boy was also hurt, but he stayed by his mother until he could walk.

There was an old woman living in a tepee not very far
from the little boy. She knew there was a child living
near her. One day she wanted to find out if the child was
a boy or girl. She placed a doll and a bow and some
arrows near the child's home. The next time she went to
look, the bow and arrows were gone so she knew the
child was a boy.

One day the boy walked to the end of a forest. He saw a lone tepee. When he was close to it a voice called, "Come in my grandchild. I have been expecting you." The little boy went in and sat down. He saw an old woman sitting opposite him. She told him to stay with her. He had the bow and arrows she had left. She taught him how to use the bow and arrows. She tied a duck head on a buckskin string and put it around the little boy's neck. She told him it would protect him at all times. His name would be Duckhead Necklace.

Sometimes he went hunting for small animals and birds. Often he was lucky and he would kill a sage hen, duck, bush rabbit, prairie chicken or other small animals. His grandmother was very proud. One day he came to a big lake. He saw a large whale swimming around. He shot and killed it with his bow and arrow. He returned to his grandmother's tepee and told her what he had done. Grandmother left saying she was going after firewood. She did not return for several days. This happened many times. Each time she came back her hair would be hanging loose and her arms and her legs were scratched and bleeding. Long ago, that is how Indians mourned for someone they had lost. Duckhead Necklace's grandmother was in mourning. In those days animals could change to people and people could change into animals. Duckhead Necklace had killed a whale. The whale he had killed was his grandmother's husband. Duckhead Necklace was very sorry. He did not know the whale was his grandmother's husband.

One day when Duckhead Necklace was walking, he came
to a tepee. From inside a voice told him to come in and sit
down at the head of a circle of young men. Each man
took turns telling him stories, hoping to put him to sleep.
Duckhead Necklace went to sleep right away, but while he
slept the duck head hanging around his neck was saying
"Yes" for Duckhead Necklace. In the Indian way, as long as
someone says yes, the stories go on and on. These young
men planned to kill Duckhead Necklace after they had put
him to sleep. The young men were actually snakes.
Duckhead Necklace woke up and heard their plan. He
grabbed one of them with his hands. Stroking the snake
from his neck down to his tail he said, "You are to crawl
on the ground always." In turn, the snakes told him never
to drink from a buffalo wallow (which is water standing
in small pools). Duckhead Necklace left. Whenever he
came to a buffalo wallow, even though he was thirsty, he
always remembered not to drink.

After many days had passed, Duckhead Necklace
thought, "It's been a long time since I was told not to
drink from buffalo wallows. I don't think anything will
happen now." When he took a drink a snake entered his
body and settled in his head. The snake did not come
out. Duckhead Necklace's body turned into a skeleton.
Still the snake stayed. The snake finally came out. When
this happened, Duckhead Necklace returned to life. He
grabbed the snake rubbing its nose on a stone, making it
flat, and he told him, "You will have a flat nose forever."

Duckhead Necklace traveled until he discovered a village. He sat on a hill and watched the camp. He noticed bears and people living together. He went down to the first tepee and went in. The people told him to sit down. They gave him something to eat. After eating, the men smoked. The people told him that at first everyone got along just fine, but now the bears took most of the meat and they left the rest to spoil. "People are starving and we can't do anything about it," the men told Duckhead Necklace.

Duckhead Necklace went to the bear chief's tepee and told him he was doing wrong by starving the people. Duckhead Necklace ordered the bears to leave and go live in the mountain forest. He also took their talking away. When the bears moved away, the people settled down to a peaceful life. After living in the village a while Duckhead Necklace decided to travel on.

Duckhead Necklace walked along until he came to another village. There the people lived with beautiful white birds. For a while, when the men hunted, everyone shared equally. As the white birds became bolder, they began taking more of the meat the men brought back from hunting. The people told Duckhead Necklace, "The birds have taken over. They eat what they want and leave the rest of the meat to spoil. People are starving."

Duckhead Necklace went to the bird chief's tepee and asked the birds to move away. The bird chief refused. He was satisfied with the way they were living. Duckhead Necklace asked several times, but each time the birds refused.

The next time the men went hunting, Duckhead Necklace went along. He changed himself into a buffalo calf and told the men to shoot him. They did. The white birds came to eat the meat the men had killed. The bird chief chose the buffalo calf. He flew down and landed on the calf. As soon as he landed Duckhead Necklace grabbed him. With his hands he stroked the bird chief from his head to the end of his tail. The bird chief turned black. -

These birds became known as ravens. Duckhead Necklace also took their talking away. The birds could no longer rule the people. The people were very happy and said many good things about Duckhead Necklace. Duckhead Necklace knew his grandmother would be proud to know he was doing good things for other people.

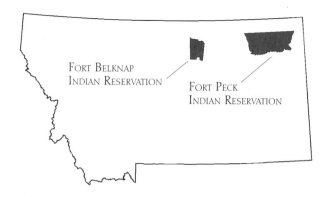

FORT BELKNAP
INDIAN RESERVATION

FORT PECK
INDIAN RESERVATION

About the Montana Assiniboine

"Known to our Canadian brethren as the Southern Assiniboine, we have lived in what is called Montana since the 1300s. Oral history tells us that we were the only Nation to use rocks to anchor or bank our lodges. The so-called teepee circles of rocks located throughout the Northern Plains are evidence of this. Archaeological evidence along the Canadian/American border in Montana is dated 1400 to 1600. Evidence exists of our ties to the Mound Builders of The Big River (Mississippi River). The evidence that the Assiniboine descended from the Yanktonai is from some Sioux in the 1600s. This Red Bottom Assiniboine Chief believes it is time to correct this wrong writing. I say we have been here since 1300s, this may be our second sojourn to this area, possibly third. Stories retained are proof of this. The Sioux story of the 1600s may have been true. Some of the Yanktonai may have joined the Assiniboines, but this story is not the beginning of the Assiniboine Nation."

Robert Four Star, Chief Buffalo Stops Four Times, RED BOTTOM ASSINIBOINE, APRIL 2003

Tribal members hunted buffalo and other game, fished the rivers and lakes, and gathered the many roots and fruit that the land provided. Active and sophisticated participants in the fur trade, they were known for pitting various fur companies against one another to further tribal interests. Small pox epidemics in the 1780s, 1800s, and 1830s ravaged the tribe, and death from disease reduced the tribe to four hundred families by 1838. Their small population led them to make alliances with other tribes, including the Cree and the Yanktonai Sioux. Today, members of the Assiniboine live on both the Fort Peck and Fort Belknap reservations in northern Montana and on several reserves in Saskatchewan and Alberta.

The stories published here have helped keep Assiniboine culture alive. Traditionally told around the fire on cold, winter evenings, stories like these were intended to help educate young tribal members about their history and culture. Children learned the stories from their elders, and, in their turn, passed them along to their children. Through this book these stories are now available to a new generation of Assiniboine children on the Fort Peck and Fort Belknap Indian Reservations and to children everywhere who are interested in learning about the traditional values and lifeways of the Assiniboine.